Handful

of
Pearls

BRIAN D'ARCY C.P.

CAMPUS PUBLISHING

First published December 1997

© This arrangement copyright Father Brian D'Arcy C.P.

ISBN 1 873223 81 1

Typesetting and design by Don O'Rourke

Printed in the Republic of Ireland by Leinster Leader Printing

Published by
Campus Publishing
26 Tirellan Heights
Galway

Introduction

It has been said that religion is for those who fear going to hell and spirituality is for those who have been there. Which means, as Kavanagh put it, that "God is in the bits and pieces of every day." It's good that God is in the bits and pieces.

There is always a need for the short, pithy, thought-provoking reflection. I know this from my articles in the *Sunday World* and from my broadcasts on BBC.

I receive over 100 letters per week. A quarter of those contain suggested reflections and quotable quotes. This is one book I did not write. I merely complied what has been written by people who have shared with me their own cuttings, reflections and thoughts. I filed them in a huge envelope, and in compiling this selection I have used only a very small percentage of what's available. In other words, beware. If this goes well, there's plenty more where it came from.

I want particularly to emphasise that I do not claim authorship of any of these. They were sent to me, mostly anonymously, to use or browse over as I wished. Where possible, I have given credit to the actual author. The vast majority have been used so frequently, and in so many places, that they must, by now, be public property. The publisher and I have made every effort to give due acknowledgement where this was possible.

The best way to read this book is to dip into it when you need to. On busy days, when God seems far away, open the book where you will. You'll find a simple view of life, of God, of religion, of spirituality and of humanity. I hope, however, it's not simplistic.

It's not advisable to read it all at one go. Anthony De Mello claimed that, should a story appeal to us initially, its true meaning will only be unearthed after we've mulled it over in our minds for at least a day. The best stories have a meaning which isn't immediately obvious.

Some of the anecdotes in this compilation are chosen precisely because they need reflecting. Others are here because they don't.

My sincere thanks to all the people who have written to me over the years and supplied me with these little pearls of wisdom. I have found them helpful. I know the readers of the *Sunday World* have, as have listeners of *Sunday with Brian D'Arcy* and *Pause for Thought* with Terry Wogan on BBC.

The proceeds of the book, if there are any, will go to help the poor. I assure you I shall not take any money from the book because I don't deserve to. I hope you enjoy the reflections. May they help your spirituality more than your religion.

Brian D'Arcy, C.P.
November, 1997

Too Much of A Good Thing

A young preacher was asked to give a sermon in a small country church. He worked hard on his sermon but was disappointed when he arrived to find that there was only one man, an elderly farmer, in the congregation.

Being asked if he wished to hear the sermon, the farmer said, "Well, if I took a bucket of meal down to the yard and only one chicken turned up, I'd feed her."

So the preacher delivered his sermon, which took about an hour and a half. Afterwards he asked the old man what he thought of it. "Well," was the reply, "if I took a bucket full of meal down to the yard and only one chicken turned up, I'd feed her of course, but I'm blowed if I'd give her the whole bucketful!"

If...

If evolution really works, how come mothers still have only two hands?

—Ed Dussault

If at first you do succeed, try, try not to be insufferable

—Franklin Jones

Paradise

An Englishman, a Frenchman and a Russian were studying a picture of Adam and Eve in the Garden of Eden. "They are obviously English," said the Englishman, "she's only got one apple but she is giving it to him to eat." "No, no," said the Frenchman, "if they are naked and eating fruit together, they must be French." "They are Russian," said the Russian firmly, "they have no clothes, hardly anything to eat, and yet they think they are in paradise."

▲▼▲▼▲▼▲

Today

Look to this day,
For it is life,
The very life of life;
In its brief course lie all
The realities and truths of existence,
The joy of growth,
The splendour of action,
The glory of power.
For yesterday is but a memory
And tomorrow is only a vision,
But today well lived
Makes every yesterday a memory of happiness
And every tomorrow a vision of hope.

Look well, therefore, to this day!

The Risk of Love

To weep is to risk appearing sentimental.
To reach out to another is to risk involvement.
To expose your feelings is to risk exposing your true self.
To lay your ideas, your dreams before the crowd is to risk
    their laughs.
To love is to risk not being loved in return.

To live is to risk dying,
To hope is to risk despair,
To try is to risk failure.

But risks must be taken
Because the greatest hazard in life is to risk nothing.

The person who risks nothing
Has nothing, does nothing, is nothing.

He may avoid suffering and worry
But he simply cannot learn, feel, change, grow, love, live.

Chained by his certitudes
He is a slave,
He has forfeited freedom.

Only the person who risks
Is thoroughly free.

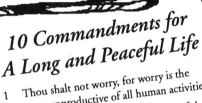

10 Commandments for A Long and Peaceful Life

1. Thou shalt not worry, for worry is the most unproductive of all human activities.

2. Thou shalt not be fearful, for most of the things we fear never come to pass.

3. Thou shalt not cross bridges before you get to them, for no one yet has succeeded in accomplishing this.

4. Thou shalt face each problem as it comes. You can handle only one at a time.

5. Thou shalt not borrow other people's problems. They can take better care of them than you can.

7. Thou shalt not try to relive yesterday for good or ill; it is gone. Concentrate on what is happening in your life today.

8. Thou shalt count thy blessings, never overlooking the small ones, for a lot of small blessings add up to a big one.

9. Thou shalt be a good listener, for only when you listen do you hear ideas different from your own. It's very hard to learn something new when you're talking.

10. Thou shalt not become bogged down by frustration for 90% of it is rooted in self-pity and will only interfere with positive action.

Suffering

A disciple told a Rabbi of Kotzk his woes: "I come from Rishin, there everything is simple, everything is clear. I prayed, and I knew what I was praying. I studied, and I knew what I was studying. Here in Kotzk, everything is mixed up, confused; I suffer from it, Rabbi, terribly. I am lost. Please help me to stop suffering."

The rabbi peered at his tearful disciple and asked: "And whoever told you that God is interested in your studies and your prayers? And what if God prefers your tears and your suffering?"

—Lucien Diess cssp

✣ ✣ ✣ ✣ ✣

Mind Your Health

Be very careful of your health. The devil employs a trick to deceive good souls. He incites them to do more than they are able, in order that they may no longer be able to do anything.

—St. Vincent de Paul

God's Will

The will of God be done by us,
The law of God be kept by us,
Our evil will controlled by us,
Our tongue in check be held by us,
Repentance timely made by us,
Christ's Passion understood by us,
Each sinful crime be shunned by us,
Much on our end be mused by us,
And death be blessed found by us.
With angels' music heard by us,
And God's high praises sung by us,
Forever and for aye.

—Traditional Irish Poem

The Duty to be Happy!

Robert Louis Stevenson suffered poor health from childhood right up until he died at the age of 44. But he never allowed illness to conquer his spirit. He felt that being happy was a duty and he faithfully followed a number of precepts to keep himself as happy as possible. Here they are:

☆ Make up your mind to be happy. Learn to find pleasure in simple things.

☆ Make the best of your circumstances. No one has everything, and everyone has some sorrow mixed in with the gladness of life. The trick is to make the laughter outweigh the tears.

☆ Don't take yourself too seriously. Don't think that somehow you should be protected from misfortunes that befall other people.

☆ Don't let criticism worry you. You can't please everybody.

☆ Don't let others set your standards. Be yourself.

☆ Do the things you enjoy doing, but don't get into debt in the process.

☆ Don't borrow trouble. Imaginary things are harder to bear than the actual ones.

☆ Do not cherish enmities. Don't hold grudges. Hatred poisons the soul.

☆ Have many interests. If you can't travel, read about many places.

☆ Don't spend your life brooding over sorrows or mistakes. Don't be one who never gets over things.

☆ Do what you can for those less fortunate than yourself.

☆ Keep busy at something. A very busy person never has time to be unhappy.

When Drinking Isn't Social Any More

There is a fine line between social drinking and drinking abusively. Social drinking is an accepted part of life, and sometimes it's hard to determine when someone crosses the line into problem drinking.

Many factors (genetic, social and spiritual) play an important role in alcoholism. If you have ever wondered about when drinking isn't social any more, looking at drinking patterns is important.

Generally, social drinkers use alcohol to relax, and to increase *good* feelings. It's easy for them to limit drinking. Drinkers start crossing the line when...

- they use alcohol to help them get through painful situations and feelings
- they defend or hide their drinking
- they can't remember what happened after a particular drinking episode
- they resent other people's advice that they should drink less
- they drink alone
- their tolerance to alcohol begins to change
- problems arise as a result of their drinking, such as being late for work frequently, getting in an automobile accident, blacking out, getting sick, or having a hangover.

If you have ever wondered about someone elses's drinking, look at them honestly. Why, how often, and in what situations do they drink? Do they drink more than others? Have they ever driven under the influence of alcohol?

Another important way to evaluate someone else's drinking is to look at how you react to their behaviour. Do you make excuses for them? If you feel someone in your circle or family is crossing the line, shouldn't you consider whether it is time to draw the line about further excuses?

If Your Partner Is An Alcoholic...

DO	learn the facts about alcoholism.
DO	develop an attitude to match the facts.
DO	talk to someone who understands alcoholism.
DO	take a personal inventory of yourself.
DO	go to a clinic or AA.
DO	maintain a healthy atmosphere in your home.
DO	encourage your partner's new interests.
DO	pass your knowledge of alcoholism on to others.
DON'T	preach and lecture to your partner.
DON'T	have a 'holier than thou' attitude.
DON'T	use the 'if you loved me' appeal.
DON'T	make threats you can't carry out.
DON'T	hide liquor or pour it out.
DON'T	argue with them when they are drunk.
DON'T	make an issue over their treatment.
DON'T	expect an immediate 100% recovery.
DON'T	be jealous of their method of recovery.
DON'T	try to protect them against alcohol.
DON'T	refer to alcohol or old drinking habits unless they do.

Letting Go

To *let go* does not mean to stop caring; it means, I can't do it for someone else.

To *let go* is not to enable, but to allow learning from natural consequences.

To *let go* is not to fix, but to be supportive.

To *let go* is not to be in the middle arranging all the outcomes, but to allow others to affect their destinies. To *let go* is not to be protective; it's to permit another to face reality.

To *let go* is not to criticise and regulate anybody, but to try to become what I dream I can be.

To *let go* is not to regret the past, but to grow and live for the future.

To *let go* is to fear less and love more.

False Prophets

Heavier-than-air flying machines are impossible.
—LORD KELVIN, President Royal Society

Everything that can be invented has been invented.
—CHARLES DUELL, Director of the US Patent Office, 1899

Sensible and responsible women do not want a vote.
—GROVER CLEVELAND, 1905

There is no likelihood man can ever tap the power of the atom.
—ROBER MILIKAN, Nobel Laureate in Physics, 1993

Who the heck wants to hear actors talk?
—HARRY WARNER, Warner Pictures, 1927

The Bones

It has been said that there are four main bones in every organisation...

The Wishbones.... those who wish somebody else would do something about the problem.

The Jawbones... those who do all the talking but very little else.

The Knucklebones... those who knock everything.

The Backbones... those who do the most of the work.

Finding The Truth

*FRED CRADDOCK, a great American preacher,
tells this personal story:*

When I was growing up in North Tennessee my father did not go to church. Once in a while the pastor would come and try to talk to him, but he was kind of rough on the minister. He would say, "I know what you fellows want down there at the church. You want another name and another pledge."

Once in a while they would have a guest evangelist, and he would come. My father would always say something like, "You don't care about me. You want another member – another pledge."

One time he didn't say it. It was in the Veterans' Hospital... I looked around the room. In the windows, on the tables... flowers... cut flowers and potted plants... I looked at the little cards sprinkled in all the flowers – from the Men's Bible Class, Women's Fellowship, Youth Fellowship, Pastor, others at the church everyone of them, the flowers and the deep stacks of cards beside the flowers from persons and groups within the church.

He saw me look at those cards. He took a pencil and wrote on the side of a kleenex box a line from Hamlet: "In this harsh world, draw your breach in pain, to tell my story." I asked, "What is your story, Dad?" And he wrote a confession: "I was wrong!"

Coronary & Ulcer Rules

*The Coronary and Ulcer Club
lists the following rules for members...*

1 Your job comes first. Forget everything else.

2 Saturdays, Sundays, and holidays are fine times to be working at the office. There'll be nobody else there to bother you.

3 Always have your briefcase with you when not at your desk. This provides an opportunity to review completely all the troubles and worries of the day.

4 Never say "No" to a request. Always say "Yes".

5 Accept all invitations to meetings, banquets, committees, etc.

6 All forms of recreation are a waste of time.

7 Never delegate responsibility to others; carry the entire load yourself.

8 If your work calls for travelling, work all day and travel at night to keep that appointment you made for eight in the morning.

9 No matter how many jobs you already are doing, remember you always can take on more.

A Father's Day Story

I once did an interview with Val Doonican. We were reminiscing about his childhood in Waterford. He was the youngest of eight children. They lived in a small house. Once, his sister, Mary, got TB. The house was so crowded that she needed a special place to herself. And to make room, his father moved out of the house, put his bed in a tool shed at the bottom of the garden and lived there for the rest of his life.

His father was somewhat fond of drink but young Val hero-worshipped him as a man who read books all the time, but kept very much to himself. Val told a story of how his father eventually had to give up work, when he got sick, and still lived on his own, in the shed at the bottom of the garden. After school Val, who was then 12 or 13, used to sit and talk to him.

He knew his father was sick but his father never told him what was wrong. One Spring evening his father asked him to go out and look in the hedges to see if the blackberry bushes were in blossom and asked him to bring him back the blooms of the bushes.

Val did as his father asked. Later while putting rubbish in the bin, he discovered, at the bottom of the bin, all the blossoms from the blackberry bushes, soaking wet and thrown in the bottom of the bin. He was horribly disappointed that his father hadn't been more appreciative of his work.

Eventually his father went into hospital. One evening Val went up to see him and his face was all bandaged. His father told him that he had a very painful illness in his mouth and that he was not a pretty sight, so it would be better if the young man never came back to see him again.

He said goodbye to him and then called him back. He had one more thing to say to him. He said: "You think I'm a hero, don't you? Well I'm not a hero at all. I've wasted my life. And the reason I'm telling you this is that when I die there will be people who will tell you that your father was a no-good waster. And I want you to be able to say, I know that because he told me himself."

Almost twenty years later, when Val was a singer, he was staying in a B & B in Scotland. He picked up a book to browse through. It was about ancient cures. And when he came to blackberries he read that, in some parts of Ireland, boiled blackberries were thought to be a cure for mouth cancer.

And it all clicked into place then. His father obviously knew he had cancer and tried to cure himself with the black berries and that's why he had boiled them and put them in the bin.

It nearly broke Val's heart. His father was long dead but he suddenly realised the kind of man he was. A silent sufferer. But a man who knew a lot about himself and a lot about what fathers should be.

To Love Is To Risk

To love at all is to be vulnerable. Love anything and your heart will certainly be wrung and possibly broken. If you want to make sure of keeping it intact, you must give your heart to none, not even to an animal. Wrap it carefully round with hobbies and little luxuries. Avoid all entanglements. Lock it up safe in the casket or coffin of your selfishness. It will not be broken. It will become unbreakable, impenetrable, irredeemable. The only place outside Heaven where you can be perfectly safe from the dangers of love is Hell.

—C.S. LEWIS

Things We Would Like To Believe

That a Church really did put up a notice:
"Pray now and avoid the Christmas rush."

≈ ≈ ≈

That schoolboys did write in their essays
that Salome danced in front of Harrods.

Facts About World Hunger

Every minute 28 human beings die of starvation. If the world's hungry were to line up in single file in front of your door, the line would continue out of sight around the world, encircling the globe 25 times.

Your dustbin probably eats better than do 30% of the people in this world.

Out of 10 children in the world today, three load their plates with large portions of food and throw away what they don't want; two get just enough to meet their basic requirements, and three fill up on bread and rice. The other two will die – one from dysentery and the other from pneumonia which they are too weak to ward off.

❊ ❊ ❊ ❊ ❊

What is Hunger?

No one put it better than Joan Pauls when she wrote:

Hunger is not that which we associate with dinner being late, or with our periodic attempts to diet. Hunger is a gnawing pain, felt every day of their lives by thousands of the children of our world. Hunger is worry and anxiety, because it means an unremitting search for food. Hunger is grief, as mothers and fathers watch their children waste away from starvation. Hunger is humiliation for the poor searching in our litter bins, feeling the eyes of judgment upon them. Hunger is fear of the future, with its unknown and consequent tragedies.

Family Ties

There was a car accident in a small town. A crowd surrounded the victim, so a newspaper reporter couldn't manage to get close enough to see.

He hit upon a bright idea. "I'm the father of the victim", he cried, "please let me through!"

The crowd let him pass so that he was able to get right up to the scene of the accident where he discovered, to his embarrassment, that the victim was a donkey.

An Irish Blessing

May there always be work for your hands to do.

May your purse always hold a coin or two.

May the sun always shine on your window pane.

May a rainbow be certain to follow each rain.

May the hand of a friend always be near you.

May God fill your heart with gladness to cheer you.

Senior Citizens

If you are not sure that you qualify as a true Senior Citizen, the following checklist may be of help:

1 Everything hurts – and what doesn't hurt doesn't work.
2 The gleam in your eye is the sun shining on your bifocals.
3 You feel like the morning after . . . but you haven't been anywhere.
4 You get winded playing cards and your little black book contains only names ending in M.D.
5 Your children begin to look middle-aged.
6 A dripping tap causes an uncontrollable urge.
7 You join a health club – and don't go.
8 You have all the answers, but no one asks the questions.
9 You look forward to a dull evening.
10 You need glasses to find your glasses.
11 You turn the lights down for economy instead of romance.
12 You sit in a rocking chair but can't make it go.
13 Your knees buckle, but your belt won't.
14 Your back goes out more often than you do.
15 You put your bra on back to front and it fits better.
16 Your house is too big and your medicine cabinet too small.
17 You sink your teeth into a steak and they stay there.
18 Your birthday cake collapses under the weight of the candles.
19 You decide to live long enough to be a problem to your kids and get your own back.

The Dragon Within

A man went to a psychiatrist. He told the psychiatrist his sad tale. He told him how everything in his life has gone wrong. How he had lost his job. How, on many occasions, he had felt like committing suicide.

Now he was in even worse trouble. He was drinking far too much. There were days, he said, when he felt like there was a dragon consuming him with a breath of fire.

He wondered if the psychiatrist could do anything about it to help him.

The psychiatrist said he could do something to help him, but there would be two conditions. Firstly, it would take him two years to do it, and secondly it would cost him £10,000.

The man was shocked at the suggestion that it was going to cost him so much money. So, he said to the psychiatrist: "I'm afraid it's time I made friends with this dragon."

There are times when we have to make friends with the dragons within us.

Slow Me Down, Lord

Slow me down, Lord.
Ease the pounding of my heart by the quieting of my mind.
Steady my hurried pace with a vision of the eternal reach of
    time.
Give me, amid the confusion of the day,
The calmness of the everlasting hills.

Break the tensions of my nerves and muscles
With the soothing music of the singing streams that live in
    my memory.
Help me to know the magical, restoring power of sleep.

Teach me the art of taking minute vacations,
Of slowing down to look at a flower,
To chat with a friend, to pat a dog,
To read a few lines from a good book.

Slow me down, Lord, and inspire me
To send my roots deep into the soil of life's enduring values
That I may grow toward the stars of my greater destiny.

Stress Points

According to the latest research, stress is a major killer in today's world.

Stress is brought about when we face more challenges than we can cope with. Not all stress is bad for us and not all stressful events have the same effect on people.

In a recent edition of the BUPA magazine, an article on stress showed that no two people react to events in the same way. Pin-pointing the causes of stress is not an accurate science. Sometimes leisure activities can add more to stress than work.

The obvious illnesses caused by stress are heart illness and cancer. But it also takes its toll on the digestive system, lungs, skin, hair, brain, immune system, relationships with others. Ulcers, eczema, asthma, baldness, muscle spasms, nervous breakdowns – all have stress as their primary cause.

Psychologists have now compiled a list of some of life's stressful events and given each a score:

- Death and bereavement .... 50 points
- Separation and divorce .... 35 points
- Moving house .... 31 points
- Marriage .... 25 points
- Redundancy/retirement .... 23 points
- Pregnancy/caring for elderly .... 20 points
- Changes at work .... 18 points
- Family squabble .... 17 points
- Promotion .... 16 points

- Changing lifestyle . . . . 13 points
- Changed working conditions . . . . 10 points
- New hobby/social life . . . . 9 points
- Change in sleep pattern . . . . 8 points
- Change in career . . . . 7 points
- Holidays/Christmas . . . . 6 points
- A brush with the law . . . . 5 points

Here's how you can add up your own stress score. If your total in any twelve month period exceeds 75 points, you have a 50/50 chance of a serious stress-related illness. For a total of 150 points, you have an 80% chance.

Work out your own destiny!

Here are a few tips for stress-busting techniques. Any of the following can help reduce stress and help you gain a new outlook on life:

- Regular exercise.
- Keeping in touch with friends and family.
- Planning and prioritising each day's activities.
- Taking your full holiday entitlement.
- Planning changes in your life on a staged basis whenever possible.
- Setting your targets in life and then aiming slightly lower – in other words, being realistic.
- Talking about your problems – bottling them up creates tension.
- Learning relaxation techniques and going out having fun.

Dear Friend,

How are you? I just had to send a note to tell you how much I care about you.

I saw you yesterday as you were talking with your friends. I waited all day hoping you would want to talk with me too. I gave you a sunset to close your day and a cool breeze to rest you – and I waited, You never came. It hurt me – but I still love you because I am your friend.

I saw you sleeping last night and longed to touch your brow, so I spilled moonlight upon your face. Again I waited, wanting to rush down so we could talk. I have so many gifts for you! You awoke and rushed off to work. My tears were in the rain.

If you would only listen to me! I love you! I try to tell you in blue skies and in the quiet green grass. I whisper it in leaves on the trees and breathe it in the colours of flowers, shout it to you in mountain streams, give the birds love songs to sing. I clothe you with warm sunshine and perfume the air with nature scents. My love for you is deeper than the ocean, and bigger than the biggest need in your heart!

Ask me! Talk with me! Please don't forget me. I have so much to share with you!

I won't hassle you any further. It is your decision. I have chosen you and I will wait – because I love you.

Your friend,

JESUS

Old Puns Never Die

Old foresters never die, they only lose their bark.
Old thieves never die, they only steal away.
Old gardeners never die, they only go to seed.
Old snooker players never die, they only go to pot.
Old prime ministers never die, they just hide in the cabinet.
Old bakers never die, they knead the dough too much.
Old vampires never die, they just grow long in the tooth.
Old dancers never die, they just go-go on for ever.
Old insurance men never die, it's against their policies.
Old cleaners never die, they just kick the bucket.
Old bank managers never die, they just lose interest.

Peace

Let nothing disturb thee;
Let nothing dismay thee,
All things pass;
God never changes,
Patience attains
All that it strives for
He who has God
Finds he lacks nothing.
God alone suffices.

Word of Wisdom

Courage is fear that has said its prayers.

If at first you don't succeed, you'll get a lot of advice.

A woman was describing her husband to a friend: "He's the kind of man who always hits the nail right on the thumb."

An expert is a man who will know tomorrow, why the things he predicted yesterday, didn't happen today.

If you don't think there is strength in numbers, consider the fragile snowflake. If enough of them stick together, they can paralyse a city.

It might be just as offensive to be around a man who never changes his mind as one who never changes his clothes.

"I sit on a man's back assuring him that I will do everything possible to alleviate his lot, except get off his back."

TOLSTOY

The trouble with many Christians is that they want to reach the promised land without going through the wilderness.

One Solitary Life

He was born in an obscure village, the child of a peasant woman. He grew up in still another village, where he worked in a carpenter shop until he was thirty. Then for three years he was an itinerant preacher. He never wrote a book. He never held an office. He never had a family or owned a house. He didn't go to college. He never visited a big city. He never travelled two hundred miles from the place where he was born. He did none of the things one usually associates with greatness.

He had no credentials but himself. He was only thirty-three when the tide of public opinion turned against him. His friends ran away. He was turned over to his enemies and went through the mockery of a trial. He was nailed to a cross between two thieves. While he was dying, his executioners gambled for his clothing, the only property he had on earth. When he was dead, he was laid in a borrowed grave through the pity of a friend.

Ninteen centuries have come and gone, and today he is the central figure of the human race and the leader of mankind's progress.

All the armies that ever marched, all the navies that ever sailed, all the parliaments that ever sat, all the kings that ever reigned, put together, have not affected the life of man on this earth as much as that One Solitary Life.

The Gift of Happiness

Learning to live joyfully is a formidable challenge. We are all trying to learn this difficult art, and some of us are better at it than others. Cardinal Newman once wrote: "I do not fear that I may have to die. I fear that I have never lived."

The Resurrection of Jesus lights our path, as does the promise of eternal life.

We should be happy, render others happy and not wait for a better world. We should be grateful for every moment in life.

Is it possible to take such advice seriously? Can we simply decide to be happy? There are some who find the idea absurd. There is so much suffering in the world that we could question whether one even has the right to pursue the goal of happiness. Yet God made us for happiness.

God waits patiently for us to understand that happiness is possible, even in the midst of pain and sorrow. Parallel to the river of sorrow flows the river of joy.

Translating this level of faith into action takes effort and imagination, but it can be done. Here are some ideas to help you on your spiritual journey:

- Look at the people you meet today with gratitude in your heart. Each of them is God's child and we are called to love them.
- Be grateful to God for every morsel of food you eat today.
- Take the initiative and make one phone call or write one letter today as a way of telling someone that you care.

- Practise some kindness today, smile more often than usual.
- Give a compliment today; point out the good in others.
- Forgive those who have offended you.

If you want to understand God's gift of happiness and joy, you must first believe in Him, not the other way around. Believe deeply and, in a leap of faith, joy will surely come to you.

Harmony

THEODORE STEINWAY, President of Steinway & Sons once noted: "In one of our concert grand pianos, 243 taut strings exert a pull of 40,000 lbs. in an iron frame. It is proof that out of great tension may come great harmony."

≈ ≈ ≈ ≈ ≈ ≈ ≈

Daring

Several years ago *The Spectator* magazine ran a contest offering a prize for the best philosophy of life that could be written on the back of a post card. The winning entry had eight words:
Love, Trust, Dare, and go on doing it.

☆ ☆ ☆

If you want long friendships, develop a short memory.

The Paradox

He was born
   But he was already begotten.

He issued from a woman
   But she was a virgin.

He was wrapped in swaddling clothes
   But he removed the swaddling clothes at the grave
   when he rose again.

He was baptised as man
   But he forgave sins as God.

He hungered
   But he fed thousands.

He thirsted
   But he cried: "If any man thirsts, let him come to me
   and drink."

He was weary
   But he is the peace of those who are sorrowful and
   heavy-laden.

He prays
   But he hears prayer.

He weeps
   But he put an end to tears.

He is bruised and wounded
   But he heals every disease and every infirmity.

He is lifted up and nailed to a tree
   But by the tree of life, he restores us.

He lays down his life
  But he has power to take it again.

He dies
  But he gives life and by his death, destroys death.

He is buried
  But he rises again.

The Guru's Cat

When the guru sat down to worship each evening
the ashram cat would get in the way and distract
the worshippers. So he ordered that the cat be
tied up during evening worship.

Long after the guru died the cat continued to be
tied up during evening worship. and when the cat
eventually died, another cat was brought to the
ashram so that it could be duly tied up during
evening worship.

Centuries later learned treatises were written by
the guru's disciples on the essential role of a cat in
all properly conducted worship.

A Prayer to Jesus Our Saviour

Lord, hold my hand,
I so need your loving kindness;
Lord, hold my hand,
All through life, in joy or grief.
Lord, hold my hand,
When I'm sick with fear and anxious;
Lord, hold my hand,
In the wonder of relief.
Lord, hold my hand,
When it's dark and storms are raging;
Lord, hold my hand,
And help me live it through.
Lord, hold my hand,
When I'm lifted, joyful, loving;
Lord, hold my hand,
When I'm trying something new.
Lord, hold my hand,
When I fail or faint or waver;
Lord, hold my hand,
For I know your love is true.
Lord, hold my hand,
When I'm lonely, weary, ageing;
Lord, hold my hand,
When there's only me – and you.
Amen.

Pearls of Wisdom

Smart people speak from experience.
Smarter people, from experience, don't speak.

○ + ○ + ○

Language is a wonderful thing. It can be used to express
our thoughts, to conceal our thoughts,
or to replace thinking.

○ + ○ + ○

Affection can withstand very severe storms and turbulence
but not a long polar frost of indifference.

— W. Scott

○ + ○ + ○

Nothing is so strong as gentleness;
nothing so gentle as real strength.

— St. Francis de Sales

○ + ○ + ○

Success in marriage is much more than finding the right
person; it is a matter of being the right person.

○ + ○ + ○

Quiet people aren't the only ones who don't say much.

○ + ○ + ○

In literature, as in love, we are astonished
at what is chosen by others.

GIVE ME

O Lord, an ever
watchful heart
which no subtle speculation
may ever lure from Thee.

Give me a noble heart
that no unworthy affection shall
ever draw downwards to earth.

Give me a heart of honesty
that no insincerity shall warp.

Give me a heart of courage
that no distress shall ever crush
or quench.

Give me a heart so free
that no perverted or impetuous affection
shall ever claim for its own.

—St. Thomas Aquinas

Mother's Day Special

There are those who think Mother's Day is just an American invention to make more money on cards, flowers and eating out. Maybe, but if mothers feel wanted and appreciated, then I'm all for it.

I came across a piece in my file recently. It was called, "Mother, I remember". It was written by a middle-aged nun who is taking care of her ailing mother. This is part of what she wrote:

When I enter the room and the loudness of the TV shocks my senses and irritation surges through me... I remember those times, Mother, when I was a teenager and you gracefully put up with my radio and stereo at full volume.

When it hurts me to see you fumble to open the milk carton with your arthritic fingers... I remember those same fingers patiently untying a knot in my shoe-lace.

When I see your eyes growing dim with age. . . I remember how those eyes would twinkle with delight at my smallest accomplishments.

When you talk on and on about things and people who are no longer a part of my life... I remember your patience when I would ask you endless questions and you gently responded to each.

When you walk so slowly that I grow impatient... I remember the walks we took around the neighbourhood when you would adjust your steps to my small feet.

When my heart skips a beat as you stumble and I quickly reach out to help you... I remember how you walked by my side, ready to catch me when I learned to ride my bike.

When you jump to conclusions and it drives me wild... I remember how gently you dealt with my growing pains when I was an adolescent.

And when you seem a million miles away, lost in your own little world... I remember best of all, when I would snuggle close to you and feel your reassuring arm around me.

Don't Quit

When things go wrong as they sometimes will,
When the road you're trudging seems all up hill,
When the funds are low and the debts are high,
And you want to smile, but you have to sigh,
When care is pressing you down a bit,
Rest if you must, but don't you quit.

Life is queer with its twists and turns,
As everyone of us sometimes learns.
And many a failure turns about
When he might have won had he stuck it out;
Don't give up though the pace seems slow –
You may succeed with another blow.

Success is failure inside out –
The silver tint of the clouds of doubt,
And you never can tell just how close you are,
It may be near when it seems so far;
So stick to the fight when you're hardest hit –
It's when things seem worst that you must not quit.

A Word To The Wise

The people to worry about are not those who openly disagree with you, but those who disagree and are too cowardly to let you know.

———❖———

It may be true that there are two sides to every question, but it is also true that there are two sides to a sheet of fly paper, and it makes a big difference to the fly, which side he chooses.

———❖———

If legs were a new invention, we would realise that they are more remarkable than the automobile or even the wheel.

———❖———

Good people learn to break big problems into small ones. The principle is as old as Aesop. In one of his fables, a farmer asked his sons to gather a bundle of sticks. The farmer tied them together with a strong cord. "Break the bundle," he asked each of them. But they could not do so. "Now, untie the bundle and break each stick separately," said the farmer. This they did, with no trouble at all.

———❖———

There are two kinds of failures – the man who will do nothing that he is told and the man who will do nothing else.

———❖———

The practical man is the man who knows how to get what he wants. The philosopher is the man who knows what man ought to want. The ideal man is the man who knows how to get what he ought to want.

The young salesman had failed to make his sale. He thought to himself: "It just proves, you can lead a horse to water, but can't make him drink." "Son," said the sales manager, "let me give you a piece of advice. Your job is not to make him drink, it's to make him thirsty."

———◆———

If you think you are confused, consider poor Columbus. He didn't know where he was going, and when he got there, he didn't know where he was, and when he got back , he didn't know where he had been.

Healing Prayer

Lord, you invite all who are burdened to come to you,
Allow your healing hand to heal me.
Touch my soul with your compassion for others.
Touch my heart with your courage and infinite love
    for all.
Touch my mind with your wisdom that my mouth
    may always proclaim your praise.
Teach me to reach out to you in my need, and help
    me to lead others to you by my example.
Most loving heart of Jesus, bring me health in body
    and spirit that I may serve you with all my
    strength.
Touch gently this life which you have created, now
    and forever.
Amen.

Hollyweds

Hardly anyone in Hollywood stays married.
But a few do. Here's how they do it:

Patrick Swayze, who's been married to Lisa Niemi for 10 years, says: "Love and friendship are the two key ingredients."

Danny de Vito, married to *Cheers'* Rhea Perlman for 21 years, says: "We never see each other, we just get together to have babies."

And then there was George Burns. As far as I'm concerned, George Burns was the funniest man on earth. So what did he say about marriage? "A great marriage starts when you get *out* of bed. It has nothing to do with bed. It's the little things. Gracie was my comedy partner and my marriage partner throughout my life. At one time, when we were married for 27 years, Gracie got all the laughs on stage but off the stage I used to make her laugh. One night she couldn't sleep so she woke me up at three o'clock in the morning and said, 'George I can't sleep – make me laugh.' So I made love to her and she laughed."

Who else but a nearly-100-year-old comedian would have got away with that!

Prayer of the Hard-of-Hearing

Blessed are they who seem to know
That lip-reading is difficult and slow.

Blessed are they that shake my hand
And write notes to help me understand.

Blessed are those who know I long
To hear voices, music and song.

Blessed are they who seem to see
When I am lost in a group of two or three.

Blessed are those who take time out
To explain to me what they're talking about.

Blessed are they who are patient and kind
That give me comfort and peace of mind.

Blessed are they who have a smile
That makes my life the more worthwhile.

Blessed are they who make it known
By faith in God's promises, I'll not walk alone.

Blessed are they who understand
As I journey to that city 'not made with hands'.

A Prayer

Lord, make me a better person,
more considerate towards others,
more honest with myself,
more faithful to you.

Make me generous enough to want
sincerely to do your will whatever it may be.

Help me to find my true vocation in life,
and grant that through it I may find
happiness myself and bring happiness to others.

Grant, Lord, that those whom you call to
enter the priesthood or the religious life
may have the generosity to answer your call,
so that those who need your help may
always find it.

We ask this through Christ
our Lord.
Amen.

God's Prayer

Most of us find prayer tough. Prayer is determined by our view of God and mankind. Why is it that we refuse to listen to Jesus telling us about the prodigal son and the host who invited everyone, even the most miserable beggar, to his table? We cling to the image of God who is ready to avenge and punish. It's no wonder it's a grim and nerve-racking experience to talk to such a God any time or in prayer. Who would ask him for anything? Who'd thank him for anything?

The apostles weren't afraid to ask Jesus to teach them to pray. He knew their weakness and He put them on the road to prayer. Here are a few tips.

Prayer is a meeting. It's a meeting with God. It is not a magic formula. It is not an escape from the pressures or worries of life. In prayer, be yourself. We should not be sad clowns who hide behind smiling masks. As long as we have our masks on, nobody ever meets us. They meet, perhaps, a successful businessman, a capable teacher, a relaxed priest, a home-loving mother, an efficient secretary. But they never see the insecure, the anxious, the sad clown we really are. It's a relief to show our true selves to someone who loves us. God does love you. It is easy to be yourself with Him.

We have to let God be Himself. We think we know God and understand Him. Somewhere in the attic of our mind we have a picture of Him with a big beard. We keep bringing it out like a dog-eared photograph from the family album. No man or woman can fully understand the

Creator of all things. He is beyond our grasp. We will never fully understand Him. So – throw away all your old notions about Him. Let God come to you as He really is, not as you would have Him. Be yourself and let God be Himself.

In that case **we can give Him all our worries.** "Come to me all you who labour and are burdened and I will give you rest." Your worries obscure your vision of God. Take God at His word and give Him your worries. *Trust Him.* You will be amazed at how relieved you will feel. Once those barriers are gone, you are ready to talk to God. Use set prayers if you want to; talk to Him if you are able. Sit in silence and say nothing, if that is what you prefer. Being in His presence is to be His.

One last tip: **Listen!** God has given you two ears and one mouth that you may listen twice as much as you speak to Him. A conversation is not only talking, but listening. You must be silent and listen to God speaking to you. You must let Jesus speak through *you* as well. Give Him a chance...

(ANONYMOUS)

Don't Play Small!

Our deepest fear is not that we are inadequate.
Our deepest fear is that we are powerful beyond measure.

❧ ❧ ❧

It is our light, not our darkness, that most
      frightens us.
We ask ourselves, who am I to be brilliant, gorgeous,
      talented and fabulous?
Actually, who are you not to be?
You are a child of God.

❧ ❧ ❧

Your playing small doesn't serve the world.
There is nothing enlightened about shrinking so that other
      people won't feel insecure around you.
We were born to make manifest the glory of God
      that is within us.
It is not just in some of us:
It's in everyone.

❧ ❧ ❧

And when we let our own light shine, we unconsciously
      give other people permission to do the same.
As we are liberated from our own fear, our presence
      automatically liberates others.

(from NELSON MANDELA's 1994 inaugural speech as
President of the Republic of South Africa)

Seeing Things

There is an old Jewish legend in which a rich but miserable man goes to see his Rabbi. The wise old Rabbi leads him to a window. "Look out there," he says, "and tell me what you see."

"I see *people*," answers the rich but miserable man. Then the Rabbi leads him to a *mirror*.

"What do you see *now*? he asks. "I see *myself*," says the rich but miserable man.

Then the Rabbi says: "Behold! In the *window* there is glass and in the *mirror* there is glass. But the glass of the mirror is covered with a little *silver*, and no sooner is a little *silver* added than you cease to see others and see only *yourself*."

Fancy Meeting You!

I dreamt death came the other night
   and Heaven's gate swung wide.
With kindly grace an angel came
   and ushered me inside.
And there to my astonishment
   stood folk I'd known on earth.
Some I had judged as quite unfit
   or of but little worth.
Indignant words rose to my lips
   but never were set free.
For every face showed stunned surprise
   – no one expected me!

Prayer in Time of Self Needs

Lord,

When I am hungry, give me someone in need of food;

When I am thirsty, send me someone needing a drink;

When I am cold, send me someone to warm;

When I am grieved, offer me someone to console;

When my cross grows heavy, let me share another's cross
too;

When I am poor, lead me to someone in need;

When I have no time, give me someone I can help a little
while;

When I am humiliated, let me have someone to praise;

When I am disheartened, send me someone to cheer;

When I need people's understanding, give me someone
who needs mine;

When I need to be looked after, send me someone to care
for;

When I think only of myself, draw my thoughts to
another.

—Father Andre Bogaert

Cultivating a Garden or Guarding a Museum?

I have grown to prefer the Christ of the light touch, the Christ who loves each one so uniquely and so absolutely that he has counted the very hairs on each head, and to be rather impatient with the Christ who has the Gospel in his safe and the Code of Canon Law on his desk. There is an image of love I once read which gives some sense of what it is that many of the disgruntled laity are saying about the nature of authority and, in a real sense, about the nature of love. Love is like grains of sand. Hold them openly in the palm of your hand and there they will stay. Grip them tightly in your fist and they will trickle through your fingers. The tighter the grip the faster they will fall.

In a sense we are and have been in the grip of an authority structure with its fist tightly closed. What it seems many of us are demanding is the open palm model...

The rate of rejection of the Church is on a steeply upward curve. Those who remain are not characterised by quiescence. Among them are, of course, those who are determined to man the barricades, to defend an unchanging Church, but equally there are those who are determined to stay and live out the famous challenge of John XXIII – to cultivate a garden, not guard a museum.

MARY MCALEESE: *Authority In The Church*
edited by Seán Mac Reamoinn

Beware of this Inner Peace!

Be on the look out for symptoms of inner peace: it is possible that people everywhere could come down with it in epidemic proportions. This could pose a serious threat to what has been, up to now, a fairly stable condition of conflict in the world.

Ten signs and symptoms of inner peace:

1 A tendency to think and act spontaneously rather than on fears based on past experiences.

2 An unmistakable ability to enjoy each moment.

3 Loss of interest in judging other people.

4 Loss of interest in conflict.

5 Loss of ability to worry (a very serious symptom).

6 Frequent overwhelming episodes of appreciation.

7 Contented feelings of connectedness with others and with nature.

8 Frequent attacks of smiling.

9 An increased tendency to *let* things happen rather than *make* them happen.

10 Increased susceptibility to the love extended by others as well as the uncontrollable urge to love them back.

A Wise King

In ancient times an Irish king was asked how he had achieved
his station in life. Said he:

I was a listener in woods.
I was a gazer at stars.
I was blind where secrets were concerned.
I was silent in wilderness.
I was talkative among many.
I was mild in the mead-hall.
I was stern in the battle.
I was gentle towards allies.
I was a physician of the sick.
I was weak towards the feeble.
I was strong toward the powerful.
I did not deride the old though I was young.
I would not speak of anyone in his absence.
I would not reproach but I would praise.
I would not ask but I would give.
For it is through these habits that the young become old
    and kingly warriors.

Answers Please!

One of my favourite writers is Frederick Buchner. His books are delightful, different and insightful.

He's credited with asking the following five questions. And if we could find the answer to these, our vision of life would be clearer.

1. If you had to bet everything you have on whether there is a God or whether there isn't, which side would get your money and why?

2. When you look at your face in the mirror, what do you see in it that you most like and what do you see in it that you most deplore?

3. If you had only one last message to leave to the handful of people who are most important to you, what would it be, in 25 words or less?

4. Of all the things you've done in your life, which is the one you'd most like to undo? Which is the one that makes you the happiest to remember?

5. Is there any person in the world or any cause that, if circumstances called for it, you'd be willing to die for?

The Shape That I'm In

There is nothing the matter with me.
I am as healthy as I can be.
I have arthritis in both my knees.
And when I talk, I talk with a wheeze.
My pulse is weak and my blood is thin,
But I'm awfully well for the shape I'm in.

Arch supports I have on my feet,
Or I wouldn't be able to be on the street.
Sleep is denied me, night after night,
But every morning I find I'm all right.
My memory is failing, my head's in a spin,
But I'm awfully well for the shape that I'm in.

The moral is this, as my tale I unfold,
That for you and me who are growing old,
It's better to say, "I'm fine," with a grin,
Than to let folks know the shape that we're in.
How do I know my youth is all spent,
Well, my get-up-and-go just got up and went.
But I really don't mind when I think with a grin,
Of all the grand places my get-up has been.

Old age is golden, I've heard it said,
But sometimes I wonder as I get into bed.
With my ears in the drawer and my teeth in a cup,
My eyes on the table until I wake up,
E'er sleep overtakes me I say to myself,
Is there anything else I should leave on the shelf.

I get up each morning and dust off my wits,
And pick up the paper and read the obits.,
If my name is still missing, I know I'm not dead,
So, I have a good breakfast and go back to bed.

—AUTHOR UNKNOWN

———◆———

Finding The Stars

Disturb us, Lord, when we are too well pleased with
   ourselves,
When our dreams have come true because we dreamed too
   little,
When we arrive safely because we sailed too close to the
   shore.

Disturb us, Lord, when with the abundance of things we
   possess,
We have lost our thirst for the waters of life;
Having fallen in love with life, we have ceased to dream of
   eternity,
And in our efforts to build a new earth,
We have allowed our vision of the new Heaven to dim.

Disturb us, Lord, to dare more boldly,
To venture on wider seas, where storms will show your
   mastery;
Where, losing sight of land, we shall find the stars.
We ask you to push back the horizons of our hopes,
And to push us in the future in strength, courage, hope
   and love.

—from St. James' Church Bulletin, New York City

Autobiography in Five Chapters

Some unknown person has written *An Autobiography in Five Chapters*. Each chapter represents a different attitude.

Chapter One
I walk down the street.
There is a deep hole in the sidewalk.
I fall in.
I am lost . . . I am helpless.
It isn't my fault.
It takes forever to find a way out.

Chapter Two
I walk down the same street.
There is a deep hole in the sidewalk.
I pretend I don't see it.
I fall in again.
I can't believe I'm in the same place.
But it isn't my fault.
It still takes a long time to get out.

Chapter Three
I walk down the same street,
There is a deep hole in the sidewalk.
I see it is there.
I fall in . . . it's a habit . . . but my eyes are open.
I know where I am.
It is my fault.
I get out immediately.

Chapter Four
I walk down the same street,
There is a deep hole in the sidewalk.
I walk around it.

Chapter Five
I walk down a *different* street.

A Blessing

May you have:

Enough success to keep you eager,

Enough failure to keep you humble;

Enough joy to share with others,

Enough trials to keep you strong,

Enough hope to keep you happy,

Enough faith to banish depression,

Enough friends to give you comfort,

*Enough determination to make each
    day better than yesterday.*

With Apologies to Darwin

Three monkeys sat in a coconut tree,
Discussing all things as they're said to be.
Said one to the others, "Now listen, you two,
There's a rumour about that *can't* be true,
That man's descended from our noble race,
The very idea's a big disgrace!

"No monkey every deserted his wife,
Or starved her babies or ruined their lives,
Or passed them on from one to another,
'Till they scarcely know who is their mother.

"And another thing you'll never see,
A monkey build a fence round a coconut tree,
Starvation would force *you* to steal from *me*.

"And another thing also a monkey won't do,
Is go out for the night and get on the stew.
Or use a gun, or a club, or a knife,
To take some other poor monkey's life.

"Yes, man descended with lots of fuss,
But brother, he didn't descend from us!"

Remember

Hospitality is making your guest feel at home,
even though you wish they were.

❋ ❋ ❋

Don't worry how great your talent is,
use what you have.

✛ ✛ ✛

Consider what would happen, if the only birds
who sang were the ones who sang the best.

✳ ✳ ✳

The hammer shatters glass but forges steel.

✢ ✢ ✢

A conference is a gathering of important people
who singly can do nothing, but together can
decide that nothing can be done.

✤ ✤ ✤

"I must do something" will always solve more
problems than "Something must be done".

After A While You Learn

After a while your learn
the subtle difference
between holding a hand
and chaining a soul.

And you learn
that love does not mean leaning,
and company does not mean security.

And you begin to learn
that kisses are not contracts,
and presents are not promises.

And you begin to accept your defeats
with your head up and your eyes ahead,
with the grace of a woman or a man,
with the grief of a child.

And you learn to build all your roads on today,
because tomorrow's ground
is too uncertain for plans,
and futures have a way of falling down
in mid-flight.

After a while you learn
that even sunshine burns if you ask too much.

So you plant your own garden
and decorate your own soul
instead of waiting for someone to bring flowers.

And you learn
that you really can endure,
that you really are strong,
and you really do have worth.

And you learn,
and you learn,
with every goodbye
you learn...

A Celtic Blessing

Deep peace of the Running Wave
to you.

Deep peace of the Flowing Air
to you.

Deep peace of the Quiet Earth
to you.

Deep peace of the Shining Stars
to you.

Deep peace of the Sun at Peace
to you.